SCHIRMER'S LIBRARY OF MUSICAL CLASSICS

Vol. 2123

The Indispensable
CHOPIN
Collection

28 Famous Piano Pieces

ISBN 978-1-4950-7157-7

G. SCHIRMER, Inc.

DISTRIBUTED BY

HAL•LEONARD®

7777 W. BLUEMOUND RD. P.O. BOX 13819 MILWAUKEE, WI 53213

www.musicsalesclassical.com
www.halleonard.com

CONTENTS

ÉTUDE
in G-flat Major

Frédéric Chopin
Op. 25, No. 9

Allegro vivace (♩ = 112)

à F. Liszt

ÉTUDE
in C minor

Frédéric Chopin
Op. 10, No. 12

Allegro con fuoco (♩ = 144)

à Mademoiselle la Comtesse Pauline Plater

MAZURKA

in F-sharp minor

Frédéric Chopin
Op. 6, No. 1

à Mademoiselle Lina Freppa

MAZURKA
in E minor

Frédéric Chopin
Op. 17, No. 2

Lento, ma non troppo (♩ = 144)

à Mademoiselle Lina Freppa

MAZURKA
in A minor

Frédéric Chopin
Op. 17, No. 4

à la Princess de Würtemburg

MAZURKA

in F-sharp minor

Frédéric Chopin
Op. 30, No. 2

à Mademoiselle la Comtesse Mostowska

MAZURKA
in C Major

Frédéric Chopin
Op. 33, No. 3

à Madame la Comtesse L. Czosnowska

MAZURKA
in C-sharp minor

Frédéric Chopin
Op. 63, No. 3

MAZURKA
in G minor

Frédéric Chopin
Op. 67, No. 2
(Posthumous)

MAZURKA
in A minor

Frédéric Chopin
Op. 68, No. 2
(Posthumous)

MAZURKA
in F Major

Frédéric Chopin
Op. 68, No. 3
(Posthumous)

Allegro, ma non troppo (♩ = 132)

MAZURKA
in F minor

Frédéric Chopin
Op. 68, No. 4
(Posthumous)

D. C. al segno senza fine

à Madame Camilla Pleyel

NOCTURNE
in B-flat minor

Frédéric Chopin
Op. 9, No. 1

à Madame Camilla Pleyel

NOCTURNE
in E-flat Major

Frédéric Chopin
Op. 9, No. 2

à Madame la Comtesse d'Appony

NOCTURNE
in C-sharp minor

Frédéric Chopin
Op. 27, No. 1

à Madame la Comtesse d'Appony

NOCTURNE
in D-flat Major

Frédéric Chopin
Op. 27, No. 2

à Mademoiselle Laura Duperré

NOCTURNE

in C minor

Frédéric Chopin
Op. 48, No. 1

à J. C. Kessler

PRÉLUDE
in E minor

Frédéric Chopin
Op. 28, No. 4

Largo

à J. C. Kessler

PRÉLUDE
in B minor

Frédéric Chopin
Op. 28, No. 6

à J. C. Kessler

PRÉLUDE
in D-flat Major

Frédéric Chopin
Op. 28, No. 15

Sostenuto

à Madame G. d'Ivry

VALSE BRILLANTE
in A minor

Frédéric Chopin
Op. 34, No. 2

WALTZ
in A-flat Major

Frédéric Chopin
Op. 69, No. 1
(Posthumous)

Lento (♩ = 138)

WALTZ
in B minor

Frédéric Chopin
Op. 69, No. 2
(Posthumous)

WALTZ
in F minor

Frédéric Chopin
Op. 70, No. 2
(Posthumous)

WALTZ
in A minor

Frédéric Chopin
KK. IVb, No. 11

Allegretto

à Madame la Comtesse Delphine Potocka

WALTZ
in D-flat Major

Frédéric Chopin
Op. 64, No. 1

à Madame Nathaniel de Rothschild

WALTZ
in C-sharp minor

Frédéric Chopin
Op. 64, No. 2

Più lento

Klindworth:

à la Comtesse Katharina Bronicka

WALTZ
in A-flat Major

Frédéric Chopin
Op. 64, No. 3

Moderato

poco a poco accel. al fine